T0050762

Draw the Circle

Prayer Journal

Resources by Mark Batterson

All In
Chase the Lion
Be a Circle Maker
The Circle Maker
The Circle Maker Video Curriculum
The Circle Maker Prayer Journal
The Circle Maker: Student Edition
Draw the Circle
The Grave Robber
If
In a Pit with a Lion on a Snowy Day
Play the Man
Soul Print
A Trip around the Sun
Wild Goose Chase

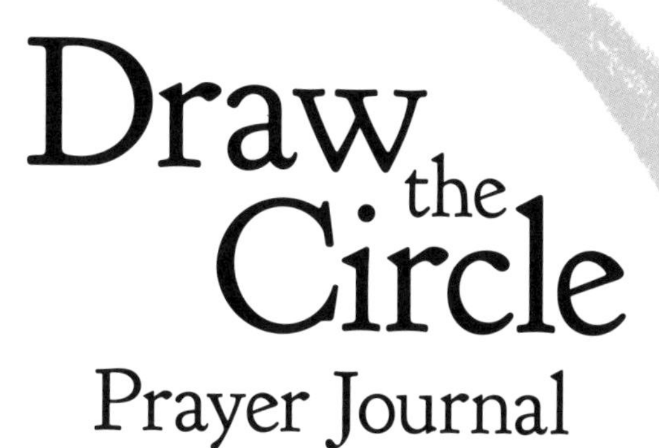

A 40-Day Experiment

Mark Batterson

New York Times bestselling author of *The Circle Maker*

ZONDERVAN

Draw the Circle Prayer Journal

Requests for information should be addressed to:
Zondervan, *3900 Sparks Dr. SE, Grand Rapids, Michigan 49546*

ISBN 978-0-310-35269-3 (hardcover)

Published in association with the literary agency of Fedd & Company, Inc., Post Office Box 341973, Austin, TX 78734.

Interior design: Denise Froehlich

Sixth printing May 2023 / Printed in Italy

Contents

A Note from the Author

This forty-day prayer experiment is going to change your life. In fact, the next forty days have the potential to dramatically alter the rest of your life. If you press into God's presence like never before, you will experience God like never before.

If you establish a prayer routine, your life will be anything but routine. You will go to places, do things, and meet people you have no business going to, doing, or meeting. You don't need to seek opportunity. All you have to do is seek God.

Please read this carefully: the goal of the forty-day experiment isn't to get what you want by the last day. In fact, the goal isn't to get what you want at all. The goal is to figure out what God wants, what He wills. Then, once you discern the requests God has laid on your heart, start circling them in prayer and don't stop until God answers.

Prayer is the difference between appointments and divine appointments, between the luck of the draw and the favor of God. Prayer is the difference between the impossible and the possible, between the best we can do and the best God can do.

There is nothing magical about forty days, but there is something biblical about it. It's the number of days Jesus spent in the wilderness fasting and praying. After His forty-day desert journey, Jesus entered into His ministry changed and filled with the Holy Spirit. At the end of this forty-day journey, you will be changed too.

My prayer for you is that you will be challenged, strengthened, and encouraged as you draw closer to the living, ever-near, profoundly good God.

The Legend of the Circle Maker

In the first century BC, a devastating drought threatened to destroy a whole generation—the generation before Jesus. The last of the great Jewish prophets had died off centuries before. God seemed to have forgotten His people. It had been such a long time since a miracle had happened that many believed miracles had never happened in the first place.

Yet, despite all the odds and God's silence, there was an eccentric sage who dared to pray anyway. His name was Honi. And even if people couldn't hear God anymore, he believed God could still hear them.

With a six-foot staff, Honi drew a circle in the dusty dirt. Then he knelt inside the circle, raised his hands to heaven, and prayed: "Lord of the universe, I swear before Your great name that I will not move from this circle until You have shown mercy upon Your children."

Honi's courage and authoritative tone were noticed by his neighbors. Without a hint of doubt, his prayer was resolute yet humble, confident yet meek.

Then raindrops began to fall. The people began rejoicing, but Honi wasn't content with just a sprinkling.

Still kneeling in the circle, Honi prayed again: "Not for such rain have I prayed, but for the rain that will fill cisterns, pits, and caverns."

The sprinkle turned into such a powerful downpour that eyewitnesses said no drop was smaller than the size of an egg. It rained so heavily and steadily that it caused flash floods. Honi still knelt in the circle and prayed a third time: "Not for such a rain have I prayed, but for the rain of Your favor, blessing, and graciousness."

The rain lessened and fell calmly and peacefully to the softened earth.

Though Honi was celebrated as a hero, some within the Sanhedrin believed that drawing a circle and demanding rain dishonored God. They threatened to excommunicate Honi, but the miracle couldn't be contested.

Honi's courageously humble prayer saved a generation that day. The story of the circle maker stands as a testament to the power of a single prayer to alter history.

No matter your story—whether you believe miracles happen or not, whether you question if God hears your prayers at all or if you're just not sure what words to say—this journey was created to help you engage with the Father through prayer. In the spirit of Honi the circle maker, my prayer is that your faith will be encouraged and that you'll experience the love of God like never before.

How to Use this Prayer Journal

The goal of this journal is to help you build a daily practice of prayer. So whatever your style is—if you prefer to write in shorthand, list in code, write in prose, or muse through doodles and colors, please do so. This book's purpose is to guide you in spending intentional time with God, using the unique voice God has given you.

This forty-day prayer journal is for the reflective writers, the scripture sketchers, the proverb doodlers, the prayer list makers. The dotted-line format was carefully chosen so that this journal could be customized to your unique prayer style, whether it is through words, drawings, or lists—or all three combined.

Each day includes a verse, a prayer prompt, space for journaling, and the circle maker's mark to encapsulate your day's prayer mantra or spiritual lesson. Blank pages are included after the forty-day experience so you may continue the journey of growing in the practice of prayer.

This book was designed to be used by itself as a guide for your personal prayer time. If you'd like a more in-depth experience, you can use this journal as a companion to *Draw the Circle: The 40 Day Prayer Challenge* devotional or *The Circle Maker: Praying Circles Around Your Biggest Dreams and Greatest Fears.*

What should I pray about? Some readers devote all forty days to praying for one specific request and continue to circle it each day. Others pray for individual requests. There is no wrong thing to pray about if you feel God has laid the request in your heart. Some readers pray for loved ones wandering in their faith, for reconciliation in a marriage, and for provision for financial needs. Some people pray for a miracle or for a dream to become reality. We've heard people pray for their own spiritual life as they ask God to draw them into deeper intimacy with Christ.

When should I pray? It's important to build a time to use this journal into your daily routine so that remembering to pray is less of a challenge. Before bedtime, first thing in the morning, or at the office during lunch are popular times that work within a daily rhythm. If it helps, we encourage you to create an appointment in your calendar or to set an alarm. If you skip a day, don't worry about it. Simply pick up the forty-day challenge again where you left off, and keep circling.

Time and time again, prayer has proven to be one of the most powerful influences in our world today. It changes history, it changes the world, it changes people, and it will change you too.

Prayer Journal Key

It can be easy to pray for a request and then forget it the next day. But as we grow in prayer, we learn that part of stewarding the prayers God has given us is remembering them until we've received an answer. As you journal your requests, you can utilize this key to code your prayers. When looking back, you can easily mark the prayers that were answered or the ones you want to keep circling in prayer.

!! Important
☆ Answered
○ Keep Circling
☐ Task to Do
☒ Task Completed
✳ To Remember

Day 1

As for God, his way is perfect:
The L*ORD's word is flawless;*
he shields all who take refuge in him.

PSALM 18:30

When Moses got impatient and took matters into his own hands by killing an Egyptian taskmaster, he thought it would expedite God's plan. In reality, it delayed God's plan and made the burden on the Israelites almost unbearable. Don't try to answer your own prayers. Stay humble, stay patient, stay focused. Bring it to God in prayer.

Identify the area in your life where you're working to answer your own prayer. Pray for the courage to surrender your concern to God and seek *His* will.

Write the name of the person or situation you are entrusting to God in the circle as you pray today.

Day 2

In their hearts humans plan their course,
but the LORD establishes their steps.

PROVERBS 16:9

God strategically positions us in the right place at the right time. It's our job to seize the divine opportunities all around us. All we have to do is follow the script of Holy Scripture and the improvisation of the Holy Spirit. We can't create divine appointments. All we can do is keep them. We can't plan God-ordained opportunities. All we can do is seize them.

List the ways you've witnessed God's divine appointments in your life. Pray for a heart that is responsive to God's promptings.

Draw a heart
in the circle today
and pray that God
will help you notice the
divine opportunities
He's placed all
around you.

"Consecrate yourselves, for tomorrow the LORD *will do amazing things among you."*

JOSHUA 3:5

All of us want to do amazing things for God, but that isn't our job; it's God's job. Our job is simply to consecrate ourselves by yielding our will to His will. We fear that if we give more of ourselves to God, there will be less of us left, but it's the exact opposite. It's not until we die to self that we truly come alive. The more we give to God, the more we have and the more we become.

Write a prayer of consecration. Reflect on any areas in your life that are difficult to give to God and ask for His help in fully surrendering your heart.

Write your name
in the circle below
as you ask God to
consecrate your life
to Him.

"This happened so that the works of God might be displayed in him."

JOHN 9:3

There is a big difference between *praying away* and *praying through*. We're often so anxious to get out of difficult, painful, or challenging situations that we fail to grow through them. Our shortsighted prayers short-circuit God's perfect plans. The primary purpose of prayer is not to change circumstances but to change us and glorify God in every situation.

Reflect on a prayer that seems unanswered. Honestly share with God your fears and concerns. Pray for endurance to *pray through* this season and ask God to show you how he wants you to grow.

In the circle, write down the prayer request you are committing to *praying through*.

"Write down the revelation."

HABAKKUK 2:2

Why is it important to journal our prayers? Because we have a natural tendency to remember what we should forget and forget what we should remember. Journaling is the best antidote—maybe the only antidote—to spiritual amnesia. Through the practice of journaling and the discipline of remembering, we can look back and chart a path between our prayers and God's answers. Connecting these dots inspires our faith like nothing else, because it paints a picture of God's faithfulness.

Consider the prayers of your heart from a year ago, a decade ago, your earliest prayers. What paths do you see from your initial requests and God's answers?

In the space below,
write or draw today's
verse as a commitment
to remember the moments
God has touched
your life.

Day 6

"Yet because of your shameless audacity he will surely get up and give you as much as you need."

LUKE 11:8

We often mistakenly think that God is offended by our prayer for the impossible. But it's the impossible prayers that honor God because they reveal our faith and allow God to reveal His glory. After all, it's not our reputation that is on the line; it's His reputation. Sometimes we are afraid of praying for miracles because we're afraid God won't answer, but the answer isn't up to us. We never know if the answer will be yes, no, or not yet. It's not our job to answer; it's our job to ask. And Jesus exhorts us to ask.

Has an impossible prayer been laid on your heart? Reflect on the request and entrust it to the One who can do all things.

Circle your risky,
impossible request in
the circle today.

They went forth and preached every where, the Lord . . . confirming the word with signs following.

Mark 16:20 KJV

When the Israelites began to enter the Promised Land, God commanded the priests to step into the Jordan river *before* he parted the water. It is counterintuitive, but God is honored when we act as if He is going to answer our prayers. And acting *as if* means acting on our prayers. After hitting our knees, we need to take a small step of faith. And those small steps of faith often turn into giant leaps. If it seems like God isn't moving in our lives, maybe it's because we aren't moving.

Journal about how your prayer life is mirrored in your daily life. Is there a step of faith that you are being called to take?

In the circle, write down the one small step of faith you will take today.

Day 8

"Speak to the earth, and it will teach you."

Job 12:8

At some point, the best we can do isn't good enough to solve our problems. That's when we need to pray and trust God to do what only God can do. After all, prayer is the difference between the best you can do and the best God can do. When we pray, the Holy Spirit will reveal things that can only be discovered in God's presence. He will reveal the secrets of His creation and the mysteries of the world to those who ask and listen. The Holy Spirit will give us not just good ideas, but God-ideas for our lives and family and work.

As you journal, bring your problem before God and ask him to reveal His wonderful mysteries to you.

If you received a God-idea or thought to help you solve your problem, write it in the circle. Or write your question and listen for God's wisdom today.

Day 9

We take captive every thought to make it obedient to Christ.

2 Corinthians 10:5

Never underestimate the power of a single prayer. Prayers have saved towns, countries, and generations. We often hear this verse quoted in negative terms, as a guard against sinful thoughts. And that, indeed, is half the battle. But this verse is also about capturing creative thoughts and keeping them in our minds. It means stewarding every word, thought, impression, and revelation inspired by the Holy Spirit. God is the great Creator, and He gives beautiful dreams to His children to accomplish.

Examine the last few days of intentional prayer. What thoughts and ideas have come to mind? How can you steward them to honor God and the dreams God has put in your heart?

Circle the one idea, thought, or truth you want to steward and remember.

Day 10

"This woman is driving me crazy."

LUKE 18:5 NLT

The viability of our prayers is not contingent on scrambling the right words into the proper combination. It has more to do with what we do than what we say. And sometimes we need to do something that seems crazy. There's a pattern repeated in Scripture: crazy miracles are the offspring of crazy faith. Just like Peter walking out on the water after Jesus, crazy begets crazy, and what seems crazy to us is normal to God. If we want to see God do crazy miracles, sometimes we need to pray crazy prayers.

Ask God for the courage to be bold in prayer. Consider if there's a crazy request you should pray or a step you should take to put your faith in action.

In the circle, write yourself a challenge to pray courageous and bold prayers.

Day 11

Devote yourselves to prayer, being watchful and thankful.

Colossians 4:2

Just like watchmen on ancient city walls, prayer enables us to see the best vantage point. Prayer is the difference between seeing the world with our physical eyes and seeing with our spiritual eyes. When we pray, we see things no one else sees. Prayer heightens our awareness and helps us see what God wants us to notice. The more you pray, the more you notice; the less you pray, the less you notice. It's as simple as that.

As you journal today, think about how prayer has changed the way you see your world, your relationships, and your work.

In the circle, write a prayer asking God to continue opening your spiritual eyes to see his fingerprints all around.

"If you have faith as small as a mustard seed . . ."

MATTHEW 17:20

Prayer is planting. Each prayer is like a seed that gets planted in the ground. It disappears for a season, but it eventually bears fruit that blesses future generations. In fact, our prayers bear fruit forever. Even when we die, our prayers don't. Each prayer takes on a life, an eternal life, of its own. We tend to want our requests answered immediately, but that isn't the way God's kingdom works. We need the patience of the planter, the foresight of the farmer, and the mind-set of the sower.

Reflect on the truth that each prayer is eternal. What kind of prayer legacy are you leaving for the next generation?

Draw a picture that illustrates this principle or write the prayer you are planting in the circle.

One day at about three in the afternoon he had a vision.

Acts 10:3

Too often we give up on our God-given dreams because we forget the simple fact that God is abundantly rich and all the earth and its resources belong to Him. Don't let fear dictate your decisions. Don't base your prayers on your limited resources rather than on God's unlimited supply. The God who gave you the vision is the same God who will make provision. The way you steward the miracles of God is by believing for bigger and better miracles. God stretches your faith so you can dream bigger dreams.

In the next pages, talk to God honestly about your fears, worries, and needs. Ask for the courage to pray bold prayers and dream big dreams, and make your request for the provision you need.

Circle your
God-given dream
in prayer or write
down the request for
provision.

"Say to this mountain, 'Move from here to there,' and it will move."

MATTHEW 17:20

There comes a moment when you must quit talking to God about the mountain in your life and start talking to the mountain about your God. Proclaim His power and declare His sovereignty. We all have impossible people or impossible problems in our lives. All we can really do is circle them in prayer. It's the only way to keep our attitude in check and allow God to do the unbelievable. The more opposition we experience, the harder we should pray. The harder we pray, the more miracles God does.

Journal about your mountain problem and turn your negative emotions into prayers for God's glory to be revealed.

Name the problem
you are praying about
today and entrust it to
God's care.

Day 15

Contend for me, my God and Lord.

Psalm 35:23

The minute you woke up today, you were already twice covered in prayer. The Holy Spirit is circling us in prayer, and the Son of God is interceding for us as well. We are double circled with songs of deliverance. God loves it when we fight for Him, but He loves it even more when we let Him fight for us. When we pray, God extends His mighty hand on our behalf. Prayer is the way we stop trying to control our problems and let God heal, redeem, and reconcile our lives. Prayer is the difference between fighting for God and God fighting for you.

Think on the fact that the Holy Spirit and Jesus are interceding for you even now. Are there any battles you should surrender and let God fight on your behalf?

The Holy One fights for
you. Illustrate or write
this truth in the circle.

"The wind blows wherever it pleases."

JOHN 3:8

Lord, surprise us. This prayer is a dangerous one to pray because we have to relinquish control. But when this prayer is motivated by a genuine desire to see God do something unprecedented, we position ourselves to experience a holy surprise. In His wisdom, God has determined that there are some things He will only do in response to prayer. The greatest tragedy in life are the prayers that go unanswered because they go unasked. If we work like it depends on us and pray like it depends on God, then God will keep surprising us.

Reflect on a time when God surprised you in some way. Remembering that God loves to bless His children in unexpected ways, ask God to surprise you and glorify His name.

Write or illustrate
today's dangerous
prayer in the circle.

Day 17

"O Lord, pay attention and act. Delay not, for your own sake, O my God."

Daniel 9:19 ESV

Prayers are rarely answered as quickly or easily as we'd like. Instead of praying ASAP (as soon as possible) prayers, we need to learn to pray ALAT (as long as it takes) prayers. It's the prayers you pray when you feel like quitting that can bring the greatest breakthroughs. When we receive quick answers, we tend to think the results are all about us. Instead, we are challenged to ask for answers that take long enough and come hard enough for God to receive all the glory. Let's look not for the path of least resistance but for the path of greatest glory.

As God never gives up on us, commit to circling your prayer for as long as it takes.

Write your request and
circle it in prayer.

Day 18

"On the seventh day, march around the city seven times."

JOSHUA 6:4

To pray or not to pray—those are the only options. Whether you've been circling your prayers for the past seventeen days or seventeen years, if the answer is *not yet*, then you've got to keep circling. It's always too early to give up! Because it's never over until God says it's over. If your cause is ordained by God, then the battle belongs to the Lord. It's His victory to win, not yours. God's timing is perfect. And as you wait, you've got to keep praying.

Today, examine the request you want to bring to God. No matter if it's an old request or a new one, if it's ordained by God, then write it down, keep praying, keep asking, keep circling.

Knowing that it's
God's victory to win,
write down your
prayer in the circle.

Day 19

"Your prayers and gifts to the poor have come up as a memorial offering before God."

ACTS 10:4

Our prayers never die. When we pray, our words exit the four dimensions of space and time because the God who answers them exists outside of the dimensions He created. You never know when His timeless answer will reenter the atmosphere of our lives. That is the beauty of prayer. We never know when His timeless answer will come or when we are the answer to someone else's prayer. When we live by faith, those memorial prayer offerings turn into praise offerings. And those praise offerings stand as a testament to God's faithfulness.

As you journal today, thank God for his wisdom and timeless answers. Pray that you can be the answer to someone else's prayer to further His kingdom.

Your prayers are never wasted but are honored as a memorial to God; illustrate this truth in the circle below.

Day 20

He [Abraham] did not know where he was going.

HEBREWS 11:8

Abraham didn't know the final destination of the journey God had called him to, but it didn't keep him from taking the first step. What's the first step or the next step you need to take in your journey? You'll never feel perfectly ready. That is why so many of us get stuck and don't take any steps at all. We keep waiting to feel prepared enough. Our failure to act on what we know God is calling us to do not only breeds doubt and discouragement; it's a form of disobedience. If you take the first step, God will reveal the second step.

In the next pages, reflect on the step you need to take. It may be small or may seem crazy, but make the decision to take it today. Pray for God to guide you as you trust His plan.

Circle the step you decided to make today and entrust the results to God.

"I'm giving you every square inch of the land you set your foot on."

Joshua 1:3 MSG

Drawing prayer circles isn't a magic trick to get what you want from God. God is not a genie in a bottle, and your wish is not His command. His command must be your wish. If it's not, you'll end up walking in circles. Drawing prayer circles starts with discerning what God wants, what He wills. And until His sovereign will becomes your sanctified wish, your prayer life will be unplugged from His divine power. And getting what you want isn't the goal; the goal is glorifying God by circling the promises, miracles, and dreams He wants for you.

As you write, ask God to reveal His will for your prayer requests. Spend a few minutes in silence as you practice listening. Ask God to sanctify your desires to match the wonderful dreams He has for your life.

Write your name in
the circle today as you
pray for God's will
to become your plan
for your life.

Day 22

"I will place a wool fleece on the threshing floor."

JUDGES 6:37

What do you do when you're not sure if your prayer request is from God or from your own mind? When God called Gideon to lead Israel into battle, he was filled with insecurity. He asked God for a sign to confirm that he was indeed hearing from God. God wants us to feel confident in what He has called us to. He often gives us answers in two ways: (1) He answers many of our questions through Scripture, and (2) He gives us a heart that can search our own motives to be sure they aren't selfish. Don't seek answers; seek God. And the answers will seek you.

Is there an area in your life or a question you have that gives you uncertainty? Lay it before the Father who knows all things and ask for wisdom.

In the circle, write down the question or issue you are praying about.

Day 23

"Wait for the gift my Father promised."

ACTS 1:4

Sometimes we must be willing to surrender something to God to receive it again. Like Abraham surrendering his son Isaac, sometimes the most precious things are the very things we lose. Sometimes God takes things away to give them back so that we know they are not ours but gifts from the Gift Giver. Otherwise, we worship the gifts rather than the Giver. Going through the process of death and resurrection teaches us to not take gifts for granted, but to steward them for His glory. When we experience the loss, we often panic. Instead, it is our invitation to press into the presence of the Giver and pray patiently, humbly, and persistently.

Have you felt the loss of a gift? Write your prayer to God, surrendering all precious things to Him and asking for His restoration.

As a memorial of surrender, write or draw all the things most important in your life in the circle.

Day 24

"The word of the Lord *came to me."*

Jeremiah 1:4

All of us have a unique voiceprint, not just physically but also spiritually. God wants to speak through you differently than through anyone else. It doesn't matter what you do; you are called to be a prophetic voice to the people God has placed in your life. The key to discovering your voice is listening to the voice of God. First, read Scripture. When you open your Bible, God opens His mouth. Second, make sure you have no unconfessed sin in your heart. If you incline your heart to God, God will incline His ear to you.

In your journal, ask yourself if there is any sin you need to bring before God. Ask the Living Word to help you listen to His words.

Lord, help me to hear your voice. Design or write this prayer in the circle.

Day 25

"I wish that all the Lord's people were prophets."

Numbers 11:29

Prayer isn't just the way we discover our own potential. Prayer is the way we recognize the potential in others. Prayer gives us prophetic eyes and supernatural insight to speak truth into the lives God has positioned in our path. When we speak words of love into someone's life, it will give them encouragement and refreshed faith. The more we press into God, the more we pray, the more insight we see. Your words have the potential to change lives by helping people discover their identity in Christ.

Consider if there is someone in your life—a friend, family member, or coworker—you should talk to, and ask God to share with you some encouragement to give them.

Write in the circle the name of the person you feel called to talk to and the message you have for them.

Day 26

Pray without ceasing.

1 THESSALONIANS 5:17 ESV

Brother Lawrence, a seventeenth-century monk, had the singular focus of spending every minute in the presence of God. He did this by turning every chore, every activity, of the day, into prayer. The simple act of praying for everybody we encounter turns the day's routine into a daily adventure. If you are a child of God, you are a priest. It's your honor and responsibility to pronounce blessing over everyone in your life. The practice of covering each minute and each person in prayer takes practice, but the difference it makes is powerful.

Praying without ceasing takes time and intention. Consider if there's a prayer tactic you can try to help you remember to pray without ceasing. Write down your commitment and ask for God's help.

Write or design today's verse in the circle.

"This kind goeth not out but by prayer and fasting."

MATTHEW 17:21 KJV

There are times when circling something in prayer isn't enough. We need to double circle it with prayer and fasting. Today's verse tells us that certain miracles only happen in response to prayer and fasting. Fasting will take us further into the presence of God. Fasting is hyper-prayer. No matter what we fast for, we need to establish a time frame and an objective. Otherwise, we're sure to quit. Maybe there's something you've been praying for that you need to fast for now. Take your prayer to the next level.

As you journal today, consider if it's time to give something up so you can lift up your prayer request. Maybe it's food, music, media, or another activity you love. Whenever you think about it during the day, replace it with prayer.

Commit to your fast
by writing down the
activity you're fasting
from and for how much
time you will fast.

Day 28

"Well done, good and faithful servant!"

MATTHEW 25:23

How many prayer requests are within our own power to answer? Yet we ask God to do what we can do ourselves and wonder why He doesn't respond. God isn't honored by prayers that are within the realm of human possibility; God is honored when we ask Him to do what is humanly impossible. There comes a time to stop praying and start acting. One of the great mistakes we make is asking God to do for us what God wants us to do for Him.

Reflect on your previous prayer requests and the requests you know the people in your life are making. Is there something you can do to help answer one of these prayers?

Circle the action you can do to help answer a prayer request.

Day 29

Sing to the LORD a new song.

PSALM 96:1

It's easy to fall into a prayer rut. We repeat all the prayer clichés we know, followed by an amen. In the same way we need variety in life, we need variety in prayer. If we're not careful, we pray without thinking—and that's just as destructive as thinking without praying. God doesn't want us to worship Him only through other people's words. Love isn't repetitive. As love grows, it needs to be expressed through new lyrics and new melodies. Get out of your regular routine and pray a new prayer to the Lord.

This time, as you journal, try a new posture or a new style. If you usually write your prayers, try drawing, doodling, or listing all the blessings you're experiencing right now.

Draw or write today's
verse in the circle.

Day 30

"If . . . my words abide in you . . ."

John 15:7 ESV

One of the surest ways to get into the presence of God is to get into the Word of God. If we get into God's Word, God's Word will get into us. It will radically change the way we think, live, and love. The Bible wasn't just meant to be read; it was meant to be memorized, meditated on, prayed, and practiced. We have to abide, to spend time, in the Word in order for God to abide in us. We cannot pray effectively if we aren't spending time with God. We have to press into His words in order to draw into His presence.

Pick a favorite Bible passage—a psalm, chapter, or verse—and slowly write or illustrate it. Be creative. Make it beautiful. List its individual promises or commands.

Write or draw the word *Abide* in the circle as a reminder.

"What do you want me to do for you?"

MATTHEW 20:32

Unlike the two blind men to whom Jesus asked the question above, many of us wouldn't know how to answer. Most of us don't get what we want, simply because *we don't know what we want.* When we make vague requests, we reveal our lack of trust in God and refuse to give Him a chance to answer our prayers. Our job isn't to worry about whether God will or will not answer our prayers. Our job is to discern the requests God has placed in our hearts and ask Him humbly yet boldly.

As you journal today, define your requests. Be specific. Are you asking for healing, reconciliation, or salvation? List it and be open to receiving God's creative answers.

Circle the specific
request you're
praying for.

Day 32

. . . and by the word of their testimony.

REVELATION 12:11

When God answers a prayer, no matter how big or small, we need to share it. It's a stewardship issue. If we don't turn the answer to a prayer into a praise, it may very well turn into pride. If we don't share our testimonies of how God is working in our lives, then others are tempted to think He isn't working at all. We rob God of the glory He deserves, and we hold out on those who need to hear the good news.

Do you have a faith-inspiring story to share? As you write, ask God who He wants you to share your story with.

Write the name of
the person you're going
to share your story with
as you pray a blessing
for them.

Aaron and Hur held his hands up—one on one side, one on the other.

EXODUS 17:12

If we are going to intercede for others, we better be sure others are interceding for us. We need a prayer covering, especially when we enter intense seasons of prayer and fasting. We will have moments when we lack the ability, strength, will, or faith to pray for ourselves. That's when we need a prayer partner or prayer circle to hold up our arms, just like Aaron and Hur did for Moses.

Reflect on the people God has placed in your life to pray and to encourage you. Consider if there's someone you could ask to partner in prayer with.

Circle the names of the people who pray for you, or the name of the individual you will ask to partner with in prayer.

Day 34

And the remnant . . . shall yet again take root downward, and bear fruit upward.

2 Kings 19:30 KJV

Every generation needs a reformation, a revival. The root of revival is prayer. For revival to come, we've got to press into the presence of God as never before and seek Him with all our heart and soul. We never know how or when a move of God might begin. But if we lay a foundation of prayer, God will build something spectacular on top of it. If we intercede like never before, God will intervene like never before.

As you write and pray today, join the timeless prayer for spiritual revival to come. Lay a foundation of prayer, inviting God to intervene in your house, neighborhood, community, and the global church.

Write today's verse
in the circle.

"Do not despise these small beginnings."

ZECHARIAH 4:10 NLT

Our heavenly Father rejoices when we take the smallest steps in the right direction. And those small steps become giant leaps in God's eternal kingdom. If we do the little things faithfully, God will do the big things. But we have to do the little things *like* they are big things. We cannot worry about what we cannot do. We must simply do what we can. If we pray and obey humbly, God will extend His mighty hand on our behalf.

In the next pages, write about the small steps you do every day in obedience. Consider if there are any other small steps God is calling you to take.

Circle the small
step you're committing
to take as an offering
to God. Or write today's
verse as a reminder that
God rejoices in your
faithfulness.

Day 36

"Store up for yourselves treasures in heaven."

Matthew 6:20

We cannot outgive God. It's not possible. The key that unlocks the joy of generosity is that what we keep we ultimately lose, what we give away we ultimately get back. The greatest legacy a person can leave is a complete surrender of their life to the lordship of Jesus Christ. If we don't hold out on God, God won't hold out on us. Every prayer we pray, every gift we give, every sacrifice we make, every step of faith we take is an inheritance left to the next generation. And our prayers live on, long after we die.

While journaling, ask God to reveal any area in your life that you have not completely given to Him. Search your heart and consider making a declaration to live a life of complete generosity.

Name the area of
your life that you're
giving to God, or
write your declaration
of generosity in
the circle.

"Whatever you bind on earth will be bound in heaven."

MATTHEW 18:18

It's important to remember that the purpose of prayer is not to get what we want but to discern what God wants. We tend to think the result is the goal of prayer. But in God's view, the process is the goal. It's not about *what* we're doing at all; it's all about *who* we're becoming in the process. The process of faithful prayer teaches us to become more Christlike. We learn to dream from an eternal perspective, to pray and intercede with more strength than is humanly possible. Through prayer, our view and understanding of God grows as we learn *who* He really is and the power of His love.

Think back before you started this journal. How are you different now? What have you learned? Who have you become?

Write your name in
the circle, asking
God to complete the
transformation He has
begun in your life.

Day 38

I will climb up to my watchtower
and stand at my guardpost.

HABAKKUK 2:1 NLT

The Israelites often built memorials in places of spiritual significance. During seasons of repentance or intense prayer, they would often return to those ancient altars to renew and remember their covenant with God. When the prophet Elijah prayed for rain, he returned to the same mountain where God had rained down fire. When you pray at the site of an answered prayer, it increases your faith. These places are like watchtowers that provide a unique vantage point into the spiritual realm. When we remember the times God answered our prayers, our strength is renewed and we discover refreshed endurance to continue praying.

What are your watchtowers and prayer memorials? Whether they're a physical location of an answered prayer, a memory, or a verse, list them in your journal.

Circle one of your prayer memorials as a testament to God's work in your life.

Day 39

"Take off your sandals, for the place where you are standing is holy ground."

Exodus 3:5

You never know when, where, or how God will invade the routine of your life. Jewish scholars concluded that God appeared to Moses in a burning bush to show that no place is devoid of God's presence, not even a bush on the far side of the desert. For that reason, they gave God the name *The Place*. God is here, there, and everywhere. Don't wait to worship God when your prayers are answered. Don't wait to worship God when you are emotionally inspired. *Here* is holy ground. *This* is a holy moment.

Instead of making prayer requests, write a psalm of thanks and praise to God or draw a picture as a creative offering to Him.

Write today's date in the circle as a reminder that on this day you experienced a moment with the Holy One—just like you can anywhere, anytime.

Day 40

"Lord, teach us to pray."

LUKE 11:1

The word *prayer* often induces feelings of guilt simply because we don't do it enough or because we feel inept when we don't know what to say. Instead, prayer should induce unbridled excitement because nothing is more potent than kneeling before God Almighty. Learning to pray is just as arduous as learning a foreign language. Don't beat yourself up over past failures or present struggles. Simply ask Jesus to help you, to teach you to pray as he taught the disciples.

Learning to pray is a lifelong process. Use the next pages to reflect on your recent prayer journey and to ask God to continue teaching you to pray today and for the rest of your life.

Write or design today's verse in the circle as you ask God to continue to help you grow in faith, humility, and prayer.

Continuing the Journey

Now that you have completed this forty-day experiment, continue growing in the practice of daily prayer on the next pages. Read a passage of Scripture to guide your thoughts and help you listen to what God is telling you, and then journal about your reflections and prayers. If at any time you feel stuck or unsure, refer back to the previous forty days for ideas and reminders.

As you continue to seek the Father "with all your heart and with all your soul and with all your mind" (Matthew 22:37), my prayer is that God will continue teaching, guiding, and leading you closer to His heart.